Finding U : The Great Alphabet Hunt

Paula Curtis Taylorson

illustrated by Janaina Galhardo

Finding U : The Great Alphabet Hunt

This is a work of fiction.

Text and Illustrations copyrighted

by Paula Curtis Taylorson ©2021

Library of Congress Control Number: 2021904860

All rights reserved. No part of this book may be

reproduced, transmitted, or stored in an information retrieval

system in any form or by any means,

graphic, electronic, or mechanical without prior written

permission from the author.

Printed in the United States of America

A 2 Z Press LLC

PO Box 582

Deleon Springs, FL 32130

bestlittleonlinebookstore.com

sizemore3630@aol.com

440-241-3126

ISBN: 978-1-954191-22-8

Dedication

Thank you to those who read to me and those who listened to me read.

He lives in an **upside**-down Greek **urn**, an **unusual** house to choose!

In a near café, some clownfish sit **under** an **umbrella**,

Waiting for their **Udon** noodles served **urgently** by an octopus Cinderella.

Where **umpteen** snails **unsuccessfully** look for an **unused** shell.

The **United Kingdom** flag stands **uneasy upon** the sand,

The local baseball match is thought **unfair**, the pitcher throws **uphill**,

The narwhal **umpire** is a sea **unicorn** who is **unable** to keep the peace,

Because **unbeknown** to him, in the crowd is a flock of **unruly Utah** geese.

He gives them all an **undercoat** of reddish-brown called **umber**,

At the **Undercurrent** Launderette, **Uri's** looking somewhat stressed,

Sitting **uncomfortably** on the wooden deck, he feels a little bit **undressed.**

Waiting for his **uniform** to dry, he's completely **unaware**,

Ursula is quite a catfish who plays the **ukulele** in a band,

She walks **upright** in high-heeled shoes, with **utensils** in her hand.

An **upsidaisy** seahorse is **unsure** what she should be,

She's an **undecided undergraduate** at the Ocean **University**.

The End

My Very Own 'U' Words:

Glossary

Page 1. **Undergrowth** : low lying vegetation or small trees growing under other trees or low to the ground
underwater : beneath the surface of the water
uncanny : not something ordinary, mysterious
ultraviolet : beyond the color violet in the color spectrum

Page 2. **Ulrich** : a boy or man's name
Urchin : a small boy or a youngster or a sea creature
U's ; a letter of the alphabet

Page 3. **Upside-**down : disorder, where the bottom part is on top
Urn : a container or a vase
Unusual : something that is not common or ordinary, not expected

Page 4. **Ulysses** : a boy or man's name
Unicycle : a bicycle with one tire

Page 5. **Uber** driver : like a taxi, a driver giving rides

Page 6. **Under** : below other items
Umbrella : a large covering

Page 7. **Udon** : a thick, Japanese noodle
Urgent : something that needs Attention or done immediately

Page 8. **Ulva s**eaweed : beds of grass underwater
Underdog Hotel : the name of a hotel

Page 9. **Umpteen** : too many to count
Unsuccessfully : not achieving a desired thing or goal
Unused : something not put to use

Page 10. **United** Kingdom : a country, England
Uneasy : restless, disturbed, not settled
Upon : to come in contact with, soon, when arrived at

Page 11. **Uri** : a boy or man's name
Usher/s : to escort or lead
UFOs : unidentified flying objects

Page 12. **Unfair** : not fair, not honest
Uphill : moving in an upward direction

Page 13. The **United** Bass : the name of the team in this book, united means to act as one, all be of the same mind or opinion
The **Ultimate** Eels : the name of the team in this book, ultimate means the best or most something can be
Unrivalled : no match for, no comparison for, no equal for

Page 14. **Umpire** : a person who rules on a game, one to settle arguments
Unicorn : a mythical horse with a horn on its head
Unable : cannot do a task or act

Page 15. **Unbeknown** : something that is not known
Unruly : misbehaving
Utah : a State in America

Page 16. **Unbeatable** : impossible to defeat, excellent
Utterly : completely, absolutely

Page 17. **Uppity** : snobbish, think they are better than others
Up : in a motion toward the sky

Page 18. **Underneath** : hidden, below other objects
Ugly : not beautiful
Unanimously : everyone is in agreement

Page 19. **Unsung** hero : unnoticed, not recognized or celebrated
Uriah Uther King : the name of the spider crab in this book

Page 20. **U-boat** : a German submarine
Upholsterer : someone who works to provide coverings for furniture,

Page 21. **Unoccupied** : no one is present, empty, vacant

Page 22. **Undercoat** : something put under something else, here it is paint
Umber : a color, reddish brown

Page 23. **Unique** : something that is not like anything else

Page 24. **Undercurrent** : the current below the surface
Uri's : a contracted word for Uri is

Page 25. **Uncomfortably** : uneasy, irritating
Underdressed : not properly or completely dressed

Page 26. **Uniform** : a formal outfit
Unaware : not aware, not able to understand or comprehend

Page 27. **Underwear** : clothing worn under outer clothing

Page 28. **Ursula** : a girl or woman's name
Ukulele : a small musical instrument

Page 29. **Upright** : erect, vertical in position
Utensils : instruments or vessels used in a kitchen, usually for serving or eating food

Page 30. **Upsidaisy** : in this book it is the seahorse's name
Unsure : not certain or confident

Page 31. **Undecided** : cannot make up one's mind
Undergraduate : lower education
University : a school of higher learning, after graduating high school

Page 32. **Underwater** : beneath the surface of the water, deep in the water
Universe : everything in the world and space
Untold : things not yet discovered or known, not yet revealed
Ularu : a very big rock in a desert in Australia
Uranus : a planet in space

Page 33. **Utterly** : completely, absolutely
Unbelievable : something that is not believable, extraordinary, not probable
U's : a letter
Uncover : reveal, make known

Paula Curtis-Taylorson Lives in Marston Mortaine England. She is a full-time secondary school teacher of English and English Literature. She was amongst the first of the initial students to graduate from the Uk's first BA (Hons) Creative Writing Program at the University of Bedfordshire.

Her first love is poetry and rhyme and she works hard to inspire and teach appreciation of the subject to all age groups. Many of her students have gone on to be successful writers.

A2Z Press LLC

A2Z Press LLC
published this work.
A2Z Press LLC is a
publishing company
created by Terrie Sizemore
for the purpose
of publishing literary works by new
and aspiring writers. All content is
G-rated. We welcome your submissions
of ideas for children's literature as well
as adult and self-help topics.
Science and medicine, holidays and
other interesting topics are all welcome.
Submit queries to sizemore3630@aol.com or
PO Box 582
Deleon Springs, FL 32130

www.ingramcontent.com/pod-product-compliance
Lightning Source LLC
Chambersburg PA
CBHW061105070526
44579CB00011B/141